Withycombe Raleigh
of Yesteryear

Part One

Sally Stocker • Elizabeth Gardner
Christopher Long • Maurice Southwell

Our families have lived in the village for generations. Working as a team we have combined our own memorabilia with local knowledge. Maurice then put the mass of information and photographs into some kind of order! We enjoyed doing it – we hope you enjoy it as well!

Our grateful thanks to all those kind people, known – particularly Richard Tarr – and unknown, who furnished us with the photographs and information on Withycombe Raleigh, and whose work may be reproduced here.

This book is dedicated to our families – past and present.

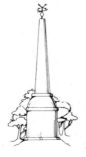

GW00502152

OBELISK PUBLICATIONS

We have over 200 Devon titles; for a current list please send an SAE to
Obelisk Publications, 2 Church Hill, Pinhoe, Exeter EX4 9ER. Tel: 01392 468556

First published in 2005 by
Obelisk Publications, 2 Church Hill, Pinhoe, Exeter, Devon
Designed by Chips and Sally Barber
Typeset by Sally Barber
Printed in Great Britain
by Avocet Press, Cullompton, Devon

©2005 Obelisk Publications

Withycombe Raleigh
of Yesteryear

Part One

"Withycombe was a village when Exmouth was a foggy dew!" or so it is claimed by Withycombe villagers, who can trace their history back to the time of William the Conqueror. With its three Manors and Quillet of Rull, the parish now known as Withycombe Raleigh extended into Exmouth. The eastern edge of the southern boundary ran from the brow of Marpool Hill down Albion Hill, then bisected the old Chapel Street as far as 'the Big Tree', which stood as a landmark outside the

earlier Exmouth Railway Station, and beyond to the Exe estuary. The principal Manor for Withycombe, called Withycombe Claville, ran from the common towards Bradham Lane. This was eventually sublet to the Raleigh family; in the course of time it came to be referred to as Withycombe Raleigh. The parish also embraced the Manors of Hulham and Broadham (Bradham), the latter being what we now think of as the original part of the village.

Limited by when photographs were first taken, this book is the first part of a visual journey through the village.

We start in about 1890 at the entrance to Phear Park, where the elegantly dressed lady stands by the gate that led to Marpool Hall. It was said the eagles on the pillars flew off when the church bells struck midnight, but they always returned by dawn!

The house shown in this small view retains the same appearance today. The mature trees help to create a peaceful scene.

Entrance to Phear Park, Exmouth.

Phear Park, Exmouth.

This sequence of Phear Park pictures shows it to have had a more park-like feel in the past. The presentation mug shown opposite commemorated the gift of Phear Park to the people of Exmouth. Until the 1960s a beautiful, ornate fountain stood in Phear Park; many have asked the question, "Where is it now?"

Below is a Coronation dinner, celebrated with an alfresco meal set out on long trestle tables in the park. Dated 22 June 1911, the photograph was taken by the talented Exmouth photographer Mr R. G. Murduck.

The impressive Marpool Hall stood at the top of Phear Park Drive, in the area now occupied by the café. It was previously owned by many distinguished families: Rodde, Hull, Aylesbury Walker, Phear and Chichester. At one time the estate was owned by Canon Henry Percy, who used it as his summer residence. He was the second son of Hugh Percy, Bishop of Carlisle, and was related to the same Percy family that holds the title Duke of Northumberland. In 1815 Collett Leventhorpe was born at the Hall. After serving in the British Army as an Officer with the Grenadier Guards, he emigrated to South Carolina and fought on the side of the Confederate Army. In doing so, he became the only British-born General to have fought in the American Civil War. As the picture below so well illustrates, this mansion was just one of many fine local buildings that have been lost since the Second World War. The board on the window ledge reads "Demolition by Joseph Ashton."

The next selection shows Withycombe Mill and its millstream. Also we have Mr Pengilley, the stableman for the Council, outside the stables at the top of Phear Park. The horses grazed on the field which later became the golf course. The small scene from about 1902, with a flock of sheep in Withycombe Village Road, shows Grange Cottages to the left and Mill Cottages to the right. Taken in about 1881, the centre picture shows Henry Long with his mother Jemima, and, looking out of the window, father Henry. In the top left view, the miller is looking downstream towards Exmouth from Withycombe Village. What an idyllic rural scene!

For many years Withycombe (or Marpool) Mill was run by the Long family. Originally it was leased from Squire Hull of the Marpool Estate. Born in 1832 into a family of millers, Henry Long later became the owner. Another member of the family, Henry John Long (1869–1953), became a local Councillor at the age of 21. He was Chairman of the Council 1911–1912, a Governor of the Grange and Exmouth Grammar School, and a manager of the Withycombe Church School. Harry Long (1915–1988) was the last Miller of Withycombe. Having succeeded his father, he ran the mill until its demolition in 1962. The picnic scene below, from 1922, shows (from left to right) Anne and Henry Long, Miss Wright (the nanny), Harry Long, Len Wilkins and Nancy Long, who later became Nancy West. At top left is the Mill Leat; the photograph beside it shows Mill Cottages, accessed by a small bridge. The building behind them is the Mill.

Withycombe Raleigh of Yesteryear – Part One

This sign on a manhole cover reads 'Marpool Mill Water Rights'. It can still be seen on the walkway leading from Moorfield Road, between the Exmouth College and the Withycombe Brook.

Below is the opposite end of the Withycombe Mill, a view not normally seen in photographs or on old postcards. Since then garages were built, and now four town houses stand on this spot.

This class from Exmouth Secondary School posed in June 1923. Dorothy Williams is third from the right in the front row, and she recalls the following names: Bert Bell, Nellie Hanger, Dorothy Phillips, Evelyn Southwell, Parker, Hayne, Goodwin, Trout and Miss Ruth Tingle, the Latin teacher. The school later became Exmouth Grammar, and is now part of the Community College.

In 1864 Lady Rolle performed the ceremony of laying the foundation stone of the new St John the Evangelist Church at Withycombe. She donated £500 towards its construction. The total cost to build the church, including the clock and organ, was £6,023.7s.

The photograph above, showing haymaking in fields at the rear of Withycombe Parish Church, was probably taken from the Hulham Road area.

The fine-looking gentleman below was the Reverend Marmaduke Spicer Shaw, the Vicar at St John the Evangelist Church, Withycombe from 1907 to 1921. During this time he suffered the loss of both of his sons; Francis Joseph (aged 23) and Marmaduke Marshall (aged 21) were both killed in the First World War. On a happier note, this rather blurred image shows some of the angelic faces of the Withycombe Parish Church Choir, circa 1935. Back row: Sam Perryman, Fred Burch. Middle row: Jack Tremlet, Ron Franks, Ron Edwards. Front Row: Bruce Pengelly, Bill Chetah, Peter Pengelly, 'Sally' Salter.

This picture is old and faded, but shows the Withycombe Hand Bell Ringers in about 1900. Included in the front row is Harry Burch, the only person who can be positively identified. It is thought that the picture was taken to commemorate the ringing of a new set of bells. Harry had been Conductor of the first peel of bells.

Monday 4 June 1934 was a very special day for Nancy Long, the youngest daughter of Mr H. J. Long; it was the occasion of her marriage to Mr Percy West at Withycombe's parish church. It was the prettiest wedding seen in Exmouth for some time.

The upper scene opposite was taken at the bottom of Moorfield Road in about 1900. It is likely that the cattle belonged to Farmer Hallet of Marpool Farm. Some of the latter's buildings still survive in Green Close. The centre picture was taken at a time when there was absolutely no need for speed bumps! Below that is a view of Porch Cottages, built circa 1600, and reputed to house the ghost of a member of the Willmot family.

The house above is Purulia; as the picture is believed to be dated about 1920, the two people in the attractive garden are probably Mr & Mrs Corbett Drewe. He was a well-known butcher in Exmouth, and had premises at The Cross.

Standing at the entrance to Raleigh Cottage, the couple in the bottom left picture are Thomas and Sarah Stocker. The photo was taken during the First World War.

With Methodism thriving in the village, it was decided to build a new larger church, so land was bought for £227.10s and plans were drawn up. A tower was included in the original design, but this was sacrificed to save some £300. The foundation stone was laid 26 June 1907, and the church opened on 6 November 1907.

Boldbrook is a typical 'chocolate box' cottage, one of the prettiest and most photographed properties in Devon. With a long history, it is said to date back to the Elizabethan era; it was the ancestral home of the Willmot family. An old black register kept at Withycombe Raleigh records the names of Thomas Wilmot and George Raleigh (elder brother of the great Sir Walter) as co-churchwardens.

The house takes its name from the Bold Brook, the stream that used to flow past the house, but is now enclosed in a culvert. We are informed that this brook is now officially a river!

In the 1870s, Burnside, shown below, was the residence of Captain Thomas Hillman Hull of the Bengal Madras Fusiliers. The house has had some notable occupants since then. In 1887 it was home to the surgeon John Dee Shapland and his family, and they were still in residence in 1914, according to the County Directory of that year. However, by 1931 Mr & Mrs J. Kenyon and their two daughters had taken over ownership. In the 1950s it was established as a guesthouse, then upgraded to hotel status. The proprietors were the Stanley family, whose daughter later started a kennel business here, but was refused planning approval to build houses in the grounds. The Council eventually used the combined gardens of Burnside and Nutbrook to develop the current estate. This was officially opened on 20 February 1960 by Mr L. M. Lees, chairman of the Council.

The above view is taken looking down through the village towards the parish church. It is a reminder of how peaceful the village used to be.

The picture below is much older, the original card bearing the date July 1909. Looking towards the Holly Tree, the thatched building on the right was one of the five Nutbrook Cottages, the scene of a disastrous fire on Sunday 30 May 1921. Built of cob with thatched and tiled roofs, they could not be saved, and 23 people were rendered homeless. The fire, first noticed at 10.30 p.m., left the children with only the clothing they were wearing, so they could not attend school the following day. The site in the 1930s saw the start of the current Withycombe Shopping area. Three shops were built: the Elm Fish & Chip Shop; H. J. Townsend, butcher; and A. J. Dymond, a general stores and newsagent. The Dymonds were a Withycombe-born family, Archie being a fine rugby player, and said to be one of the best kickers of a ball in Devon. He and his brothers formed the backbone of the village team.

Alf Burch and his son, Fred, are seen here making their way, in rustic fashion, through the village.
Below, a grand greeting is being given to Major Morrison Bell, possibly returning from the Boer War. The County Directory for 1914 provides the information that Major Arthur Clive Morrison-Bell MP lived at Harpford House, Ottery St Mary, and also had the luxury of a London town house at 7 Great Cumberland Place. The white cottages to the left of the picture were demolished in 1938. The land on which they stood now forms part of the pub's car park.

Sarah Stocker, the lady in the bath chair, is featured in both the photos on this page. Above she is pictured with Peter, Harry and Pauline Stocker outside the Holly Tree. The other prominent building is the premises of Thomas and George Stocker, a saddlery business. This building was demolished in the late 1940s. With a strong family presence in the village, between 1901 and 1938, Peter and Nelly Stocker were the licensees of the Holly Tree and brewed their own beer, using water from a natural spring in their grounds. The picture below is outside this pub and also features Alf Pyne, Nelly, Peter, Harry Stocker.

Withycombe Raleigh of Yesteryear – Part One

Like many other pubs, the Holly Tree had its own token system, which enabled customers to buy beer.

Below are Withycombe Raleigh School Group 2, circa 1915. Back Row: Mr Benstead (Headmaster), Frank Hillman, Les Perkins, Bob Dunne, Bert Phillips, Fred Coles, Bert Denner. Middle Row: ? Palfrey, Doug Wilmore, Bob Watkins, Reg Chetah, Ron 'Polly' Perkins, Lionel Carpenter, Ron Snow, Bill Snow, Tom Harding, Harry Stocker. Front Row: Ida Stuart, unknown, Rene Stuart, Hilda Willsman, ? Bellamy, Joy Oliver, Gladys Long, Margery Burridge.

To the left is PC George Leach, who was the policeman at Withycombe from 1931 to 1937.

To the right is Helen Buttle, in about 1920, dressed up for Empire Day. This was a very important item on the school calendar; it was celebrated with games and was a 'fun day' for all pupils.

The picture below was taken in about 1930 and shows a group of girls rewarded for their sporting achievements. A framed portrait of a feather has been presented to them. Those present included Kathleen Wilson, Nancy Willmot, Susie Tucker, Diane and Margarite Beavis, Barbara Sampson and Jean Pyne.

The top picture opposite is from a May Day, sometime during the 1930s. Included within this picture are Diane and Margarite Beavis, Iris Lindsey, Gwen England, Susie Tucker and Tony Greenaway. The middle picture, opposite, was taken in the grounds of the previous Withycombe Vicarage at Brookhayes; the church can be seen in the background. This is now the site of Brookhayes Close and shows the successful Withycombe School Pupils with their trophies won at the East Devon District School Sports 1931. In the photograph are: Tony Moger, Arthur Andrews, Muriel Denner, Douglas Hookway, Mixie Saunders, Audrey Pyne, Wally Pyne, Jerry Hookway, Dorothy Paver, Geoff McCormack, Eileen Andrews, Terry Andrews, Pat Wilson, Albert Perryman, Eileen McCormack, Nancy Willmot, Leslie Willmot, Jean Newton, Jack Tremlett, Roy Edwards, Olive Franks, Susie Tucker, and Jamie Eveligh. Headmaster of the school was Mr Benstead. The picture at the bottom dates back to 1930, when these May Day Mermaids (Diana & Margarite Beavis, Violet Edwards. Gwen England and Jean Pyne) appeared in the village.

The theme for this Withycombe carnival entry in 1930 was based on nursery rhymes: "Ride a Cock Horse" – Betty Bowerman; "Jack and Jill" – Cynthia Kiff (Jack) and Joan Newton; "Mary, Mary, quite contrary…" – Iris Lindsey; "Little Miss Muffet" – Pam Kiff; "Little Jack Horner" – Pam Osbourne; "Little Boy Blue" – has not been identified.

Quoits is an outdoor target game in which rings – usually iron and weighing about $5^1/_2$ lb (2.5 kg) – are cast toward a peg stuck in the ground. Having certain similarities to bowls, the game probably was an extension of horseshoe pitching. In this picture from about 1900, Walter Pannell is featured along with at least three or four members of the Lindsey family. They were the acknowledged experts of the local brickyard industry, having worked at the Watery Lane Brickyard. The family supplied foremen for both the Withycombe and Salterton Road Brickyards. Another well-known local character, by the name of Wilson, is also said to be in the picture.

Another enterprising carnival entry! Here we see Joan Newton as a cobweb. In the background, it is just possible to see the brickyard chimneys with the foreman's cottage to the right. This photograph was taken at the home of dressmaker Mabel Pannell, who made the costume.

The top right picture is of the Burch family of Withycombe, as listed in the 1901 Census: Harry and his wife, Bessie, their daughter, Kate, and their two sons, Alfred and Harold. At that time they were unaware that young Jack Burch would, sometime in the future, become another family member. Harry was a successful businessman and became a contractor, moving into the family home where Harold ('Tiny') ran Moorside Dairy; Alf continued to work with the cattle and smallholding, later branching out to run the village general stores.

Below is the cover of a Coronation programme, the small print revealing some familiar names.

These are the Withycombe Rugby Football Club's players for the 1925/26 season. Many of them have been recognised and are thought to be: (standing) Peter Stocker, Ed Lindsey, Fred Dymond, Paul Perkins, Fred Franks, Ben Edwards, Fred Lindsey, Harold Bradford, Morgan Willmot, Alf Dymond, Harold Burch, Alf Burch, Herman Stuart; (sitting) ? Doran, Frank Cole, ? Doran, Donald Rowsell, Philip Rowsell, both Club Presidents ? Bolt, ? Packer; (squatting) Lionel Smith, Walt Tucker, Bert Clarbull, Jack Edwards and Archie Dymond.

The present club was formed in 1924, with early games having been played at the old Hill 60 ground. This was reached by crossing the brook via stepping stones beside the Country House pub. The field on which they played was part of Marpool Farm and is now the site of Moorfield Close. The team later moved to Marcus Road and then Palmer's Field, now occupied by Dene Close. Moving to Raleigh Park in 1934, the land had formerly been a market garden owned by Mr Raleigh Willmot. Originally this sports ground had been prepared for a hockey club operating from Exmouth. However, it folded, and the rugby club took over. Rugby had also been played by Withycombe teams prior to this, on land which is now Phillips Avenue. These were the Annual Good Friday 'friendly games' against Littleham. Friendly? You must be joking! This picture was taken at Nutbrook, home of the Rowsell Family.

"Let's have a charabanc ride." This group of hardy souls was going to Cheddar Caves on 27 June 1928. Standing in the middle of the vehicle were lifelong friends Mabel Pannell and Alice Norton. It is likely that about twenty or so postcards were printed at Cheddar, the organiser or coach driver making the necessary arrangements. We wonder what was in the cans on the running board?

Dated about 1930, the picture above was taken in Burch's Field. This lay behind the Moorside Dairy, between Henson's Field and what was the school playground. Standing are Fred Cole, Jim Stuart, Harry Willmot, Jack Franks, George Franks, whilst sitting are Jack Burch, Peter Dymond, and George Willmot.

There is some debate as to who possessed the last working horse in the village. The candidates include Fred Burch, shown below working with his horse, Madam, Mr Bond of Bradham Lane, and Mr Andrews of Brixington.

Seen in this top photo are Walter James Pannell and Rosina Perriam, who were married at Withycombe on 21 November 1891. For a number of years he worked for Major General James Harwood Rocke, CB as a gardener at Tenerife, later Rocke House, in Trefusis Terrace. His employer was the nephew of the late Revd Thomas James Rocke, MA, who held the living of Littleham, Exmouth from 1843 to 1877. During this period Major General Rocke was a constant visitor to the town, which he adopted as a place of permanent residence on retiring from the Army.

Taken in about 1906, No. 1 Jubilee Cottages (now 138, Withycombe Village Road), is shown at top right. Twins Mabel and Maud Pannell were born here. Their mother was a dressmaker who ran a shop; cotton and odds and ends can be seen for sale in the window of the front room. Over the door was the wording "Pannell, licensed to sell tobacco, cigars & stationery".

The next picture is of yet another Exmouth Carnival winning entry, the tractor having pulled a 'First Prize' float.

However, there was little time to savour the success; the float was whisked back to the Withycombe Brickyard to be dismantled ready for work the next morning. This photo shows Eddie (Nibs) Burch on the tractor with Ivan Turner, Harry Willmot, Fred Morrish and a few friends.

Withycombe Raleigh of Yesteryear – Part One

Walter James (Jim) Pannell and family moved here to live with his widowed mother. In the Kelly's Directory of 1889, she was listed under the heading of 'Commercial' as "Pannell, Mary (Mrs) Laundress". The family can still remember the copper boiler in the scullery and the hooks in the high ceiling.

Jim Pannell, in his spare time after work, had an allotment in the Cranford area of Salterton Road and his own large garden, where he used to produce fruit and vegetables for sale in the shop. The shop traded until 1941 when, with life dictated by wartime coupons, the decision was made to close it.

The picture here shows Rosina Pannell in the doorway of her house watching her daughter Maud, in chequered dress, standing at the gate.

The picture here is of the Withycombe Brickyard, as seen from the high ground of Pound Lane. It clearly shows the flooded quarry pit and the 100-foot-high chimney stack. At the top centre of this view are the houses of Bradham Lane. The row of trees is now the site of Moorfield Road.

T. Abell & Sons took over this quarrying business in 1918, and used the traction engine seen below for transport. The enterprise grew apace and the output was increased to 3,000,000 bricks a year. However, times changed and the yard closed in the 1930s. Jewson's Builders' Merchants and Palmer's Garage now occupy the site.

Much has been written about the Bystock Estate, and a few lines here cannot do it justice. Older residents often spoke of the Bryce family of Marley who, from 1906 to 1929, owned both the Bystock and Marley Estates. Mr Frederick Coleman Hunter occupied Bystock, rebuilding it after the disastrous fire of 1903 (see overleaf for details), which had happened before he moved in. He was President of the Devon County Cricket Club from 1923 to 1930; the cricket ground at Bystock was the scene of many pleasant encounters, in which not only local teams but also touring sides played.

Major Cecil Pellow Bradshaw, who had married Miss Violet C. Duckworth-King (daughter of Col Sir Dudley Duckworth-King) of Wear House (now the Exeter Golf & Country Club), Exeter, took up residence at Bystock in 1929. He was well known as a breeder of Jersey dairy cattle, and also renowned as a big game hunter, having done a great deal of shooting in India and South Africa. He presented his collection of 'trophies' to the Royal Albert Memorial Museum, Exeter.

Below are Tom & Nell (Helen) Wright, the latter being shown twice. They lived opposite the forge of blacksmith Billy Morse, on the other side of the brook; Nell must have been a familiar sight with her laundry cart. We believe she also did the laundry for the hospital. Imagine her journey up Marpool Hill!

Most local people had thought of Bystock as one main house, on the site of the current building, but on reading reports of FIRE AT ST JOHN'S COTTAGE in the papers of 26 December 1903, a different story emerges: *An alarming fire of considerable proportions, and the existence of which the people of Exmouth were ignorant until late in the evening, broke out at St John's Cottage, on the Bystock Estate on Monday afternoon. The building, a large and imposing one, prettily situated, and containing upwards of forty rooms, is scarcely 200 yards distant from Bystock House. A portion of it is Elizabethan architecture, having a thatched roof, the remainder being quite a modern addition. The house has not been occupied since last March, and was being redecorated at a cost of £1,200, Mr F. Grace, the builder having the contract. It is understood locally that the premises were let to a gentleman and his family, who were due to take possession at Lady Day next.*

The fire occurred just before 2 p.m. in the thatch covered portion, and it is presumed – though the actual cause is quite unknown – that it originated through the action of a blowlamp used by a

Withycombe Raleigh of Yesteryear – Part One

painter to remove the old paint from a window. The roof was very soon ablaze, and a strong breeze only hastened the work of destruction, which the efforts of all the available workmen on the Bystock Estate were powerless to diminish. Supt Pett, of the Exeter Fire Brigade, was communicated with, and in a few minutes nine men and the steamer, drawn by four horses, were speeding to the scene of the conflagration. On their arrival, just before 5 p.m., the older portion of the house was completely ablaze. The water supply was limited, but the damming of a brook on the estate provided an additional supply, and three powerful jets played continually on the flames for two hours, in which time the fire was mastered, and the destruction of the modern additions averted. The original portion of the dwelling however, consisting of twenty rooms, was completely burnt out. The fire smouldered for hours after being got under control, and it was not until the early hours of Tuesday morning that the firemen were able to leave the place. The property belongs to Mrs J. P. Bryce, and the damage is estimated at £2,000.

On a less exciting note, the picture opposite shows the roof of the chancel at the lovely St John in the Wilderness Church being restored between 1922 and 1936.

On this page are the Revd Gregory and Mrs Bateman. He was vicar at Withycombe Parish Church 1925–1936. During this time, the Church Hall was built, the bells were re-hung, and the Church Path from Hulham Road was laid. The highlight of his work was the restoration of the ancient church of St John in the Wilderness. For nearly two centuries the old church had been a crumbling, overgrown, ivy-clad ruin. Herbert Read, the builder, started the work in 1926 and continued it into the following year. Further work recommenced in 1932, this ancient church being completely restored by 1937, just before the abdication of Edward VIII. The total cost was nearly £6,000. The church is unique in that there are two memorial bosses to the uncrowned King Edward VIII in the chancel roof.

The picture shows ivy growing up the tower, at a time when the church was neglected, seldom used and in disrepair. St John in the Wilderness was built sometime between 1381 and 1435 and was originally dedicated to St Michael. Withycombe Raleigh was then part of the parish of East Budleigh; the church was probably built to serve the farming communities and outlying cottages. By the late 17th century, the area had become too remote from the population of Exmouth and Withycombe, and so in 1720 the new chapel was built in the centre of the village on land next to the Holly Tree Inn, only to be demolished in 1864 when the present parish church was built.

We finish part one of our journey around Withycombe with this revealing aerial view. It was taken in 1929 and the key is as follows: A–Park Road, B–Lyndhurst Road, C–Marpool Mill, D–Withycombe Church, E–Withycombe Methodist Church, F–Withycombe Brickyard, G–St John's Road/Bradham Lane, H–Pound Lane, J–Raleigh Park, K–Mudbank Brickyard, L–Bapton Farm.